Guidelines For Effective Business Communication

Online Trainees

Content

This course provides clear guidelines for Effective Business Communication.

Module 1

Effective Business Writing

Introduction

Planning your writing

Write the first draft

Edit the document

Design the visual format and layout of the document

Check the final draft

Module 2

Effective Business Presentations

Introduction

Understanding the components of oral communication

Factors to consider when preparing a presentation

Structure of an effective presentation

Visuals

Preparing the environment

Presentation skills – assessment rubric

Presentation skills – coaching checklist

Pitfalls of business communication

Module 1 - Effective Business Writing

When was the last time you read a business document and understood it first time? Chances are you had to re-read it carefully – assuming of course, you didn't just throw it away in frustration!

As we all know from personal experience, most business communication is difficult to interpret. The main reason for this is that there are no globally agreed standards for clarity and readability: everyone is doing their own thing, and the result is a mixture of different styles, layouts and structures.

In this module, you will learn how to communicate effectively in the business environment.

Most of us sit down, write until we have said everything we can think of, and then send off the document.

The end result: a document that is too long, too jumbled, too wordy, too disorganized, unfocused, and, ultimately, unread.

The human brain processes information and thoughts in complex ways. One part of our brain enables us to put thought into words. Another part enables us to sequence ideas into a logical order. Two different brain functions are involved. The practicality is therefore that you cannot write and plan at the same time. Still another part of our brain enables us to critique and evaluate. This means that you cannot write and edit your own work at the same time either.

Accomplished writers know that planning takes more time than any of the other steps in the writing process.

Let's have a look at how these steps apply to business writing.

Before starting on this module, complete the questionnaire below to assess your current business writing abilities.

Yes / No / I don't know

I always keep my audience in mind when I write

I have no problem with the basics: grammar, spelling and punctuation.

I know the difference between active and passive construction.

I choose simple words to communicate clearly.

I make it a point to state clearly the specified purpose of letters, memos and reports.

I recognize and avoid business clichés and jargon.

I ruthlessly edit everything I write.

I am confident I can communicate persuasively.

I find it easy to write business communications

Planning your writing

If business writing is to be effective, you must know whom you are writing to, and why.

You must also know what you want to accomplish, and you must use language and tone that are appropriate to the purpose and the reader. You should include everything your reader needs to know and no more. In other words: plan first, write second.

Clarify The Purpose: Why Am I Writing?

One of the most common problems of business writing is the failure to make the purpose of the communication clear. This means that the reader is not sure what they are meant "to get out of" your business communication.

Ask yourself the following: Why am I writing this?

What does my boss/colleague/client/customer need to know?

Identify the recipient: To whom am I writing?

Identifying your readers assists you as the author of a specific letter/memo or report to target the major group of readers for a document. It enables you to discover what the readers need to know in order to perform their jobs better, or, in order to increase their knowledge about a specific subject. It also assists you to determine what the readers will do with the information they have read.

Who Is The Recipient?

Try to answer this question in as much detail as you can. For in-house reports, this means identifying your readers by name and position. This sort of analysis helps get you out of the void of trying to communicate to nameless, faceless readers. It is much easier to write if you have some definite ideas about whom you are writing for.

What is the educational background of the recipient?

With this question you are trying to determine if the reader shares a common educational background with you. Ask yourself if you could participate in a discussion on the topic with the reader on an equal level. This question helps define your readers' identity.

What is the professional background of the recipient?

This question helps you to determine whether the reader shares similar experiences with you. It is important because it enables you to determine the appropriate vocabulary to use in the document, how much background is required, and how much definition of terms and concepts the reader needs.

These recipient identification questions are important because they enable you to get a picture of what the projected recipient is like. Writing to a person you can visualize is far easier than writing to an unidentified person. Beyond that, identifying your recipients forces you to start thinking about how the information should be organized.

Once you have identified the recipient; you can start planning your ideas and choose an appropriate format for communicating your ideas.

Remember:

This is a business communication. Write what they need to know, not what you want to say.

What Kind Of Business Communication Should You Write?

Identify the type:

Should it be a formal memo or a casual email?

Should you write a brief review or a full report?

Should you write a short memo describing your request or a full proposal?

What is appropriate for this industry or environment?

What terminology and conventions are appropriate to the business function and industry?

Gather ideas and information from a wide variety of sources.

When you are wrestling with the complex question of what to include in the document, it is useful to brainstorm and mind map ideas.

A mind map helps us to visually organize our ideas. It has the following characteristics:

There is a core concept in the centre.

There are important themes radiating from this one concept.

Each of these themes is broken down into branches showing sub-division of the theme.

These sub-divisions in turn, are broken down into more detailed branches.

Next to each branch, write a word that summarizes the idea.

This allows you to group similar ideas together, apples with apples and pears with pears.

It is easy to make connections between ideas by joining them with arrows.

Ideas occur in no particular sequence. They can be captured as they come to mind.

Use a mind map to put all your thoughts on paper, to group similar ideas together and to show connections between them.

You can also use coloured markers and circles to identify main categories of ideas.

Then decide which of the points really need to be included in the document.

Remind yourself of two things you have already done:

What is the purpose of the document?

Who is the reader?

As you go through the points, cross out items that are not relevant. Be ruthless. Only include things that your reader needs to know.

Now take the remaining ideas and organize them into a logical sequence.

Check that point A leads to point B which leads to point C which leads to conclusion.

Now assess all the information from any relevant sources. You will also need to check information for accuracy, bias, stereotypes and other offensive details.

Write The First Draft:

Using the plan you have created, you can now write the first draft of the document. Write the complete document, and then edit. People who teach effective writing stress "free writing". This means writing without stopping. The rationale is that the physical act of writing itself activates the creative part of your brain.

In business writing, take one point at a time and start to write. Commit to paper everything that passes through your mind about that topic. Don't stop to evaluate what you have written, just keep writing. If you follow your planned outline, your thoughts will be focussed on the purpose of the document.

Handy Hints

Work during your best hours:

If you are faced with writing a report or other document, try to work on it when you are at your freshest. Unfortunately, it is human nature to put off tasks we don't like. So, often, when we have to write reports, we leave them until the last minute when we are too tired to think clearly.

Create a conducive environment:

Shut the office door.

Don't take phone calls.

Clear your desk of everything else.

Don't allow interruptions. Set an alarm for a specific time – e.g. 15 minutes. Write without stopping until the alarm goes off.

Then take a break. Set the alarm again and so on until the final draft has been completed.

Select The Appropriate Format And Structure

The business letter:

Business letters should be well structured and the message must be conveyed clearly.

Letterheads:

A letterhead provides the business name, address and telephone number at the top of the page. In addition, there might be an international telephone, fax code and email address.

The names of the directors may appear as a footer or footnote of the letter. The quality of paper when printing letterheads is important.

Layout of addresses:

The full address of the writer followed by the date in full, should be written at the top right hand corner of the letter. It is preferred that blocked format is used. No punctuation is used when you apply the blocked format.

When writing a business letter, the name and address of the person or organisation to whom, or, to which the letter is addressed, should be written on the left hand side of the letter. This address must be in line with the last line of the address in the right hand corner of the letter.

If the title of the addressee is known, it is often preferable to use the title e.g. "The Principle", "The Editor", or "The Manager". This address also has no punctuation marks.

Complementary salutation and ending:

In cases where the surname of the addressee is unknown, use one of the following:

Dear Sir

Dear Sirs

Dear Madam

Dear Sir/Madam when the gender is unknown

When the surname of the addressee is known, use one of the following:

Dear Professor Smith

Dear Dr Coetzee

Dear Ms Roux

Dear Miss Lourens

Dear Mrs Brown

Dear Mr Gordon

You may end the letter with:

Yours faithfully

OR

Yours sincerely

Your letter must be signed. Your Initial(s) and surname must be stated clearly below the signature. A title or a woman's marital status is normally indicated after the surname.

The reader will automatically presume that the writer is a man if the initials and surname only appear at the end of the letter.

If you have an official title, it can be written beneath your name. Remember that the salutation and the endings begin at the margin and there are no punctuation marks.

The Subject Heading:

The subject heading is optional. However the advantage of including a subject heading is to enable the reader to see at a glance what the letter is about. Remember to write the subject heading below the salutation, against the left hand margin.

The first letter of the initial word, and of all other significant words, is written with a capital letter. The whole subject heading is underlined. You can write the entire subject heading capital letters, but then underlining is not necessary.

Example:

Dear Sir

Application for Teaching Post (underlined)
Or

Dear Sir,

Application for teaching post (in bold)

The concluding paragraph:

A business letter does not have a lengthy concluding paragraph. After providing all the necessary information, you can simply conclude your letter as follows:

"If you need any other information, I shall be pleased to discuss the matter with you".

The concluding sentence provided above is only an example of how a business letter (such as an application for a position, or a request for an overdraft) can be ended. The way you conclude your letter will depend on the type of letter you have written.

Envelopes And Addressing Envelopes

The correct way to address an envelope:

The title of the recipient

The name of the recipient

The name of the business organisation

The postal address

The name of the post office or suburb in capital letters

Allow a separate line for each line of the address.

Hints:

Addresses on envelopes should be typed in the middle part and towards the right hand side of the envelope. Do not write anything in a space of 1cm from the bottom or in the top right hand corner.

When window envelopes are being used, care should be taken with the folding of the paper and the positioning of the address so that the full address is visible.

Special instructions, such as "for the attention of", should be typed 2 lines above the address.

Other special instructions such as "Express" or "Registered" should be typed in the top left hand corner of the envelope.

Internal Memos

Memorandums are internal documents within a company and are used for inter-departmental or inter-personal communication. They are usually referred to as memos in business circles. A memo is a fast, efficient way to communicate with co-workers or readers.

A memo stays within in the company. Readers of the memo evaluate your communication skills on the basis of how efficiently you can convey a message to the reader.

There is usually a standard form drawn up by each organisation. Therefore using a memo is time saving.

It is important to take note of the following four important aspects of the format of a memo:

Types of memos:

Memos differ in length and content and can range from a brief, informal note to remind a colleague of a meeting, to a multi-chaptered, confidential report by a diplomat on matters of international importance.

Memos are classified according to their destination within the organisation, and also in accordance with the direction in which information is transferred within the organisation.

The following memos can be differentiated:

Office memos

Inter-departmental memos

Memos between head and branch offices

By utilising memos, messages can be conveyed upwards, downwards and across.

Functions Of Memos

Memorandums are used in business to remind the reader of important matters.

A memo can be utilised to convey narrative and reflective instructions to the reader. It can also form part of the office routine to respond to a request, or to follow up on a telephone conversation, or to initiate/propose an action.

Memorandums remain as permanent, written records and once the Intended people have read them, they should be signed and filed. Memorandums keep the channels of information within the company open, and convey messages clearly.

Style Of Memos

Memorandums should be concise, precise and unambiguous. When writing a memo, you need to be clear, coherent and logical in your arguments. Make sure that the purpose for writing a memo, the target audience and the context is clear, in relation to the activity.

Avoid careless spelling and grammatical errors. Use full sentences and do not use telegraphic style.

Memos are more informal than business letters or reports, but the degree of informality will depend on the writer/recipient relationship and the nature of the memo.

Like business letters, memorandums are also written in the active voice:

"I feel…"

"I have enclosed the report"

DO NOT USE PASSIVE VOICE:

"It is felt…"

"Requested report has been enclosed"

Paragraph numbering or using bullets can assist you to convey the message in an organised manner and it also makes cross-referencing easy. There is no excuse for incomplete sentences.

Format Of The Memo

Memos have three parts: the heading, the sub line and the relevant information that needs to be communicated.

Good memos must be brief, unambiguous, yet polite. They ask for information, or convey messages. They can convey personal instructions. A brief note may contain only one sentence. Memos need not be signed since the sender's name appears at the top of the memo.

The actual message of a memo can be written in various ways. The memo may also consist of only one or two sentences. No matter what form the message is on the memo, it must always be clear and concise.

Information provided in longer memos includes the reason for writing the memo, relevant detail and recommendations. It is often necessary to make use of a brief sub-heading to distinguish between the various aspects. The paragraphs are numbered in accordance with the decimal system. It is acceptable to initial longer memorandums.

Emails

When you reply to an email message, make sure you include part of the original message.

This is called quoting. Quoting helps the reader identify which message you are replying to.

To save the reader time, make sure you delete all parts of the message that do not directly relate to your reply. After reading a message, you can add comments and then send the message to a colleague. You can print a message to produce a paper copy of the message.

One way to ensure that your emails generate action and impact is to get into the habit of quickly reading through them to see if they pass the G.R.E.A.T. test. This acronym is a handy way of remembering the following key areas for composing email messages that produce timely results in a stylish way:

Goal:

What is the purpose of email? Have you told the receiver why you are sending the email or are you giving them the facts without a background or context?

Relevant Facts:

Have you provided enough upfront information? Are you assuming that the recipient knows the details of what you are talking about? Have you provided them with the information they need to respond appropriately to the communication?

Emotional Tone:

What mood have you set for this email? Often people send emails thinking about what to say, not about how they sound.

Action:

Have I made a specific request? If you want the recipient to take some specific action by a certain time, let them know.

Timeframes:

Have I told the reader by when I need a response or action taken? In today's busy world, you cannot assume that your timeline for action is the same as the reader's. If you need a response or action taken by a certain date, be specific about it in your message.

Reports

There are various types of reports e.g. accident reports, reports of social functions, news reports, and business reports.

A report can be defined as an account given, or a opinion formally expressed after investigation or consideration. It is a formal way of communicating and is frequently used to make decisions.

A report is based on research/knowledge regarding a specific subject. It conveys and presents the message clearly, logically and in a readable way. A report is written with a specific audience in mind and always in the past tense. It is written without personal pronouns e.g. I, You, We and presented in very specific terms e.g. it should not go beyond the terms of reference, the topic, or the conditions, on which the reference is made.

Guidelines On How To Write A Report

The main heading must be clear and must state the nature of the report. It must be short.

Terms of reference refer to the background of the report. It states under whose authority the report has been undertaken and what the specific objectives of the report are.

Procedure provides details of the methods of research and the treatment of data for the report.

The author explains what the findings or objective facts, resulting from the research, were.

In conclusion, the author interprets the findings of the report.

Usually the author makes recommendations indicating a course of action to be followed.

A report should include a signature, including the typed name of the report author, and his/her position. This information is important for the reader to assess the validity of the conclusions and the recommendations.

It is important to include the date since reports may be referred to much later after it was written and there may be more recent research available.

Presenting a report too late is of little use. The decision maker will need your information to be on time before proceeding. Therefore, establish early on, when and how often you will be presenting your reports. Also find out the length of the reports, so that you can determine the time that you will spend writing it and presenting it verbally.

Structure Of A Report

Title

Introduction: It leads the reader into the story and presents the main message, the common thread that will connect all ideas that follow.

The opening catches the reader's attention.

It is followed by the main idea. Reading the introduction gives the reader a clearer idea of what to expect in the rest of the report.

The Main Body

You are now discussing each idea and show how one idea leads to another.

Each idea is presented in a separate paragraph.

Recommendations: If relevant, recommendations can be included.

Edit the document:

Drafting, editing and revision of the first draft are vital. The successful writer never overlooks this important process.

Editing and revision are the next steps in the process of writing business letters/memos or reports. For most, the idea of what constitutes a good report or memo is only a gut reaction to one's own work. Something seems good or something seems to need more work. While this process may succeed for some, it is difficult to develop the skills that are required to make accurate criticisms of one's own work.

Editing text:

The process of editing can be quite difficult and tedious. You need to check the grammar, diction, sentences and paragraph structure to ensure overall consistency of your business letter/memo or report.

Proper Word Usage

Proper word usage is another problem for business people. Often words sound the same, are spelt differently and mean something completely different e.g. stationary/stationery, effect/affect. You have to ensure that you are using the correct spelling to convey the correct information.

Style

There are a few writing rules you should obey:

Kiss:

Keep it short and simple

Short:

A sentence should not have more than 20-30 words. Say things in a few words. If you can cut out a sentence or some words, do so.

Simple:

Do not try to impress with your command of English. Say it as you speak. Use technical language only when necessary.

Use Active Voice

Instead of saying: "John was interrupted by Pete" rather say " Pete interrupted John".

Tone:

It not only matters what you say, but also how you say it. Words that help the reader to see a picture make a stronger impression. Be convincing. Write facts not opinion. Do not offend or exclude anyone. Be polite. Use appropriate language.

Active and passive voices:

When you add information or write more complicated sentences, a writer often loses sight of the basic sentence components – subject and verb. The order that the words are presented in and how the writer selects the subject and verb, also affect the reader's understanding.

For clarity and good sentence structure, it is best to arrange a sentence in the following order – subject, verb and object. This order is referred to as active voice construction.

An example is:

The President ….. called a ….. meeting ….. of the board of directors.

(subject) ……. (verb) ……. (object)

The passive construction of a sentence is less clear than the active construction. Active voice is the preferred construction for business communication. An example of the same sentence in passive voice is:

A ….. meeting of the Board of Directors was …… called by the …… President.

…..(subject) …….. (verb) ……… (prepositional phrase)

Transitions

Transitions in your writing are another necessary component of sentence structure.

Transitions are used to show how ideas relate to one another. They can bridge sentences and paragraphs, leading the reader from one thought to another smoothly. They can also help keep the reader's attention.

Example:

In spite of the shipping delays, the customers were completely satisfied with the product they received. Consequently they ordered another five tons to be delivered next month.

The phrase "In spite of the shipping delays," explains the problem that had to be rectified keep the customers happy. "Consequently" indicates that the following sentence resulted from the previous statement.

The following table highlights types of transitional words and phrases.

Type	Examples
Example	For example, for instance, as an illustration, thus, further
Time	First, second, third, next, after, afterwards, then, meanwhile, when, soon, tomorrow, today, still, again, yet
Addition	Also, furthermore, moreover, besides, too, as well as
Result	Thus, therefore, consequently, because, hence
Contrast	However, but, nevertheless, to the contrary, in contrast, still, unless, although
Other	Certainly, truly, clearly, in fact, surely, likewise, indeed, in conclusion

Inappropriate Language

As the author to a defined audience, you must be aware of inappropriate or potentially harmful influence that can be implied by the language spoken by individuals and the definition they give to words.

The following can be regarded as inappropriate use of the language:

Jargon:

Jargon is speech, signing or writing used by a group of individuals who belong to a particular trade, profession, or any other group, bound together by mutual interest. For example the jargon of the law profession or the medical profession.

Jargon is useful when used within a trade or profession, but when it is used to exclude listeners/readers/viewers from interaction, it is potentially hurtful or even harmful.

Insensitive choice of words:

Writing a text is not a haphazard task that just happens. The words which you as a writer choose, go a long way in helping the reader toward making choices and decisions. Words and phrases need to be chosen in such a way that it is not insensitive and harmful to the reader. Avoid swear words and words that can be interpreted as chauvinism.

Slang:

Slang is referred to as casual, very informal speech/signing, using expressive and informal words and expressions. Slang is usually related to age or social group rather than to trade or profession. It is used to stress an identity for those in the know and to exclude those who do not know the terms. For example: Words to describe money, grown-ups, police and activities.

Offensive or incorrect register:

Register is a variety speech or signing used by a particular group of individuals, usually sharing the same occupation or the same interests. You as speaker, writer, presenter, and signer must choose signs, words and images that are easily understood by the target listener. Remember that the pitch must suit the purpose.

Design The Visual Format And Layout Of The Document

Meaningful title:

The report or other document should have a meaningful title. The title should instantly tell your reader what the report is about. The title should also contain a complete thought. So, if your report is based on the need for people not to work through lunch because it is bad for productivity, call it:

Working through lunch is bad for productivity

Rather than

Working through lunch

Or

Productivity in the workplace

Table Of Contents:

This breaks the report down into logical, digestible sections.

Make your point right away:

Making your point as early as possible is critical. It allows your reader to:

Understand the report quickly.

Act on it quickly – or pass it on to someone else.

Read the rest of it productively, instead of wondering where it is heading.

Long reports need a summary:

Any report longer than a few pages needs a summary; this can be as short as one paragraph or as long as one page. Write it on the assumption that the reader won't read any further; that way, you will focus on what he needs to know, rather than what you would like him to know.

For a short report, your point is the main heading:

For a report that is one or two pages long, your point is invariably the main heading – and whatever sub-text you may think is necessary.

Make your headings descriptive:

A heading should be descriptive – e.g. it should describe what is about to follow.

Headings can unscramble complex text:

Headings are particularly useful in unscrambling long or complex paragraphs so that key points stand out.

For example:

Before

A concern expressed was whether writing documents in plain English would impose substantial costs on public companies. The response to this was that while there may be additional costs initially, these would, in all probability, be modest. Moreover, they would diminish as firms learn plain English principles.

After

Concern: Will writing documents in plain English not impose substantial costs on public companies?

Response:

There may be additional costs, but these will probably be modest and should diminish as the firm learns plain English policies.

Structure:

Break the text up into clear, logical sections.

Differentiation:

Use different font sizes and styles to differentiate main points and sub points.

Without overdoing it, use different font sizes and styles. This relieves the monotony of the page and makes it easy to pick out key words and phrases.

Isolate specific pieces of text and highlight them by playing around with:

Boldness of text

Capitals

Italics

Different fonts

Remember to use capitals sparingly. They are okay in titles and headings, but never in entire sentences.

Compare the following examples:

CALLING ALL MBA HOPEFULLS

If you are a senior employee and wish to apply for the Chairman's MBA scholarship you must first attend a preliminary interview. The following time slots have been scheduled for the interviews:

Monday - 6 March - 10h00 - Boardroom 1

Tuesday - 7 March - 14h30 - Boardroom 5

Friday - 10 March - 10h00 - Boardroom1

Calling all MBA Hopefuls

If you are a senior employee and wish to apply for the Chairman's MBA scholarship you must first attend a preliminary interview. The following time slots have been scheduled for the interviews:

MONDAY - 6 March - 10h00 - Boardroom 1

TUESDAY - 7 March - 14h30 - Boardroom 5

FRIDAY - 10 March - 10h00 - Boardroom 1

Use A Clean, Airy Layout

It makes your text stand out and allows you to highlight key points.

A lot of white space is important in making a report inviting and user-friendly. It makes headings and graphics stand out, and enables you to draw attention to key paragraphs. In other words, it makes your documents readable – and that is what it is all about.

An Example Of An Effective Report Is Provided Below:

Report:

How using plain language saves you money

You get fewer queries, fewer errors and waste less time.

1. Phone enquiries plummet.

US computer company Allen-Bradley simplified the user manual for its programmable computers. Phone enquiries through the call centre fell from 50 per day to 2 per month.

2. R375 00 saved in phone calls.

General Electric simplified its software manuals. Users of the new manual made about 125 fewer calls per month. This translated into savings of between R22 000 and R375 000 per year.

3. Productivity gains R400 000.

Federal Express simplified all ground-operations manuals. The average search time for information dropped 28% and the chances of readers finding the correct answer rose by 50%. The money saved in the first year was at least R400 000.

4. Error rate down from 55% to 3%.

After UK Customs and Excise simplified its lost baggage forms, the error rate on returned forms fell from 55% to 3%. The new form saves R33 000 a year in staff time.

5. Police slash thickness of procedures book.

The Greater Manchester Police Department reduced its procedures book from 750 000 words to 60 000 words by rewriting it in plain language. The result: quicker turnaround time on cases.

6. New form saves R400 000 in staff time.

The UK Defence Ministry simplified a travel form used by over 750 000 people every year. The new form cut the error rate by half and also reduced processing time. It cost R12 000 to simplify, and saves R400 000 a year in staff time.

Check The Final Draft

The final step in the process is to print and check the final draft of the document you have produced. Since it is difficult to check and edit documents on the computer screen, it is better to complete the final edit on a hard copy of the document.

Use the following checklist to assess the final copy of the document. Where necessary, make corrections and modifications, recheck the document and send it to the relevant person or people in the correct format (electronic or hard copy).

Self Assessment: Written Report

Use this checklist to assess the report you have written.

1. Has the report met organisational, sector and legislative requirements?

2. Is the purpose of the report clearly stated?

3. Is the report suitable for the target recipients?

4. Has it met the client's needs?

5. Is the information accurate and unbiased?

6. Has the information been accessed from a variety of relevant sources?

7. Is the structure appropriate e.g. letter, email, report?

8. Effective use of layout?
Text type
Format
Bullets
Numbering
Headings
White space

9. Appropriate grammar conventions.

10. Plain language.

11. Syntax
Long sentences
Incorrect use of passive construction

12. Spelling

13. Punctuation

14. Focal Point
Visuals
Graphs
Tables
Flow charts
Diagrams

15. Errors and accuracy

16. Is the report meaningful and logical?

17. Is the report culturally and aesthetically sensitive?

18. Is there evidence of a first draft of the report?

Module 2 - Effective Business Presentations

Communication between two people or between one person and a group of people, can be broken down into three categories. The weighting of each category, in terms of information sent and received, is as follows:

Body Language	60 – 80%
Voice Tone/Inflection	20 – 30%
Words	7 – 10%

An effective speaker understands that for a message to be received, understood and remembered by an audience, more depends on how you say things than on what you say.

How you say things relates to your delivery style which includes the use of:

a) Body language – gestures, movement, stance, posture, dress and appearance.

b) Voice tone and inflection.

c) Audience involvement techniques such as your use of visual aids.

What you say refers to the actual words you speak – the content, which if logically constructed, will lead to a convincing and persuasive delivery. If the "what" part of your delivery is solid and comes from your heart, then the cadence is allowed to flow more naturally.

Although words account for only 7 – 10% of your communication, they are still vitally important.

For Example:

If you are insincere and unenthusiastic about your subject or the words you are using, your body language and voice tone are going to reflect these negative feelings.

It is the effective combination of 'how' and 'what' that enables you to deliver powerful presentations.

The Use Of Body Language During Presentations

Body language plays a major role in communication because information to the human brain is received:

87% - Through the eyes
9% - Through the ears
4% - Other senses

Gestures

Make a conscious effort to improve your use of gestures when presenting. If you fidget, the audience fidgets. If you look relaxed, the audience relaxes. When you enjoy your presentation, so does the audience.

Add emphasis and meaning to your words through "talking" with your hands, arms, face and body.

Never use gestures that might offend your audience, e.g. wagging, pointing or jabbing your finger and command gestures such as hand held out, palm down. Rather talk with "open" palms – palms turned upwards.

Movement

Move away and out from behind the lectern area and move towards your audience (into the "U" of a U-shaped table).

Add variety: avoid predictable movement between the same two points, especially between the lectern and your visual aid equipment.

Move naturally and with purpose, but avoid pacing. It is important that you have the ability to stand still. In fact, this is preferable to pacing, rocking or swaying. However, purposeful movement is extremely powerful, so do not become bolted to one spot on the floor permanently.

At the beginning and end of your presentation, make a point of moving towards your audience. Never retreat backwards at these stages in your presentation.

Stance And Posture

Your stance and posture is responsible for conveying your credibility, authority and presence more than anything else in your body language. So maintain good posture – shoulders back, head upright, feet slightly apart, knees relaxed and keep your weight firmly and equally balanced.

Learn to consciously relax your shoulders to avoid hunching and remain constantly aware of this.

Eliminate your "royal stance" and "hands-in-pocket" stances. Stand with your hands at your sides, as this is the most open and neutral position you can adopt.

Avoid poses such as hands on hips, arms folded across the chest and rocking backwards and forwards.

Your posture and stance must always convey that you are in control. Maintain your vitality and enthusiasm, never let the audience believe that your resources are getting low.

Dress

Dress comfortably for the occasion. Rather be overdressed than underdressed – a rule of thumb is to be as well dressed as the best dressed person in the audience.

Avoid flashy, outlandish or extreme clothing and jewellery. They will distract the audience – this also applies to make-up and hair styles.

In a business environment, it is best to present in dark colours because they give you presence and power.

Using Your Voice

More is communicated in the tone of your voice than the actual words you say.

The voice must be free and responsive to reflect what you think and feel. It must be as interesting as what you have to communicate. It should always be able to surprise.

Variety in your voice will keep the audience interested in what you are saying. Vary your pitch, volume and pace. It is better to talk on the slightly faster side than too slowly, because people's brains work at a very fast pace.

Work at improving the tonal quality of your voice. Place inflections on words for greater meaning.

Let intense emotions such as anger, joy, excitement and sadness are heard in your voice. Do not overdo it or be insincere, be natural but let yourself go and let it come from the heart.

Breathe correctly and make yourself aware of the occasions when you don't. Remember, your voice comes from your diaphragm, so keep your throat open and let your voice out, do not push it.

Clarity is absolutely essential, so do not mumble or slur your words. Concentrate on pronouncing everything clearly.

Words

Keep It Simple

Ideas expressed simply are often the most clear and powerful.

Always try to reduce the number of words needed to clearly express your ideas – all audiences young and old like presentations that get to the point.

The most important skill you need to develop is the ability to create word pictures for the audience. Use vivid, descriptive and concrete language because human beings are visual creatures.

Include pauses to emphasise points, separate ideas and points, and ensure that your message comes across clearly.

Never swear or blaspheme. It takes away your professionalism.

Avoid "talk" language such as "to be honest", "to be frank" or "with all due respect". People translate these common phrases to mean the opposite of what they actually say.

Consider your audience and do not use words the audience does not understand. If you do use slang or acronyms, make sure they are understood, and never use too many.

Use pauses to replace non-words like "umm" "ahh" "OK" and other repetitive phrases.

Factors To Consider When Preparing A Presentation

Your Objective:

Why are you doing this presentation? What is the purpose?

Is It To:

Persuade and convince?

To inform?

To entertain?

Does your audience have an obvious interest in your objective? Is this what they are expecting from you?

The Audience:

How much do they know about the subject?

What information do you have on the audience?

What is their objective in listening to you?

What are their needs? Can you prioritise these needs?

Who is the key decision maker? Who else has influence?

What is their background?

Do you have supporters and/or opposition amongst them? If so, who?

What is their culture and what is their first language?

Demographics/other relevant information?

What is the result or action that you want from your audience after listening to you? Here you must be specific. Think of the next logical step in you negotiation, educating, informing or sales process.

The benefits to your audience if they take the action or experience the result of your proposal. The benefits are the justifications and motivating factors for your arguments/proposal/information and you should always have these defined, no matter what you are trying to achieve.

The physical Surroundings:

Will you be speaking indoor or outdoors?

Is the venue big or small?

What audiovisual equipment will be available?

Structure Of An Effective Presentation

Once you know what you want to talk about, why, to whom and where, it is time to start preparing the material for the presentation.

Then you need to organise the material into logical, coherent presentation. For a presentation to be effective it needs the following:

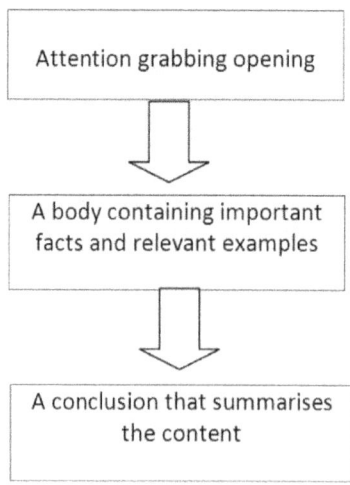

40

The Opening: Get The Audience's Attention

The opening includes the following aspects:

An opening statement that must gain the attention and interest of the audience. The opening statement is the first thing you say and it happens before you set the scene. It must give a hint of what the presentation is about and set the scene for what is to follow.

In your opening statement you can arouse curiosity with a thought provoking question, a frightening or interesting statement, or shocking fact. Whatever its form, your opening statement must cement interest between you and the audience. Do not state the obvious such as:

"It's a fascinating age we live in."

"The rapid rate of change is dramatically altering the way we do business."

Setting the scene could include a preview, stating the topic of your address, or stating your objective/viewpoint in a different way. Again ensure that the scene you set is of interest to the audience, so that they realise you are delivering a presentation that relates to their needs. Avoid describing exactly where you are going – a detailed agenda for instance – rather let your presentation unfold as you progress.

It is not necessary to acknowledge all dignitaries unless there is very strict protocol. Just warmly thank the person who introduces you and greet the audience with the time of day – such as "good morning".

Novice presenters very often lose their audience by waffling through an aimless and long introduction. Just get on with it.

When you begin your presentation, do not rush into your introduction. Catch your breath and start a little on the slow side. Your opening manner should be relaxed and congenial.

Know The Introduction Well

This is when you are going to be the most nervous, and, it is during the first 4 minutes that the audience creates their first impressions of you. Knowing your opening really well gives you that extra confidence when you begin.

The Body

As you arrange your points in logical order, critically examine each point for its contribution to your whole presentation. Discard these points that do not relate to your main purpose.

Keep your outline flexible. Each key point shall be "self sufficient" and should be able to stand on its own, so that if you run out of time, you are able to discard points as you speak.

Create change of pace. Let the audience relax every now and then. Contrast and release will give your points more impact and keep your audience with you.

Check that you are not using too many "I's" and not enough "we's".

Ensure that your content gets more exciting as you build towards your conclusion. Check that you are putting your most exciting content towards the end of the body.

Conclusion

The conclusion is the section most likely to be remembered by your audience. The quality is therefore vitally important. The conclusion is the climax of your delivery, where you must re-enforce your objective. You will achieve this by stirring the emotions and feelings of the audience as well as their minds.

An effective conclusion has three components:

The call to action: Where you clearly state what it is you want your audience to do or experience as a result of this presentation. This is the whole purpose of your presentation so make sure you spell it out clearly and with conviction without talking down to your audience.

Summarise the main points.

A closing statement that must be rousing, memorable and given in a positive, confident manner.

Do not tail off. Go out in a confident and measured manner. Do not rush it or end with an embarrassed sigh. Smile no matter how badly you think you have done.

Do not include humour in your closing, because, you want to leave the audience with a strong impression of your objective. In a business presentation it is better to leave them thinking and doing.

If you have a question and answer session at the end, then have a final closing after this session.

Coping With Nervous Tension

Nervousness is something which effects just about anyone who is called on to speak in public, but the secret is to let your nervous energy work for you. Somebody once said that nervous speakers are good speakers – fear and tension sharpen their strategy so that they do their best.

Breathing and relaxation exercises can help you to keep your nervousness under control.

Be yourself

Prepare adequately

Rehearse and rehearse again

Dress appropriately

Allow only positive thinking

Breathing Exercises

Inhale slowly and as deeply as possible. Hold your breath for 5 seconds, then exhale all the air slowly through the split between the teeth. Breathing like this a few times before you get up to speak will slow down your heart beat and allow you to breathe normally afterwards.

Visuals

We rely on visual sense extensively. In order to maximise what your audience understands, remembers, listens to, and, most importantly, does about what you are saying, make use of visuals during your presentation. However, many presenters rely so heavily on their visual that in effect, the visuals give their presentation for them. Visual aids should support, not dominate a presentation.

Some Common Mistakes

Reading the visuals

Putting too much information on the visual and /or making them too busy with far too many different colours.

Having too many visuals

Revealing too much information all at once without co-ordinating what is seen with what is said. When this is done the audience does not obtain the all important combination of seeing and hearing to improve retention.

Not having enough light on the presenter

Despite their importance, visual aids cannot substitute for an effective speaker talking from the heart. You are the presentation and visual support should never replace you.

Composing Your Visuals

Use pictures, charts and graphs. Not just numbers and words. The more graphical your visuals the greater the impact they will have.

Use visual ideas from books, newspapers, magazines or anywhere else that you find useful. A humorous visual can be very effective.

Illustrate relationships, contrasts and trends through graphic comparisons. For example: In a bar graph make all the bars one colour except the one you want to highlight.

Keep to the same format in headings, background colour, text and bullet colours etc. Otherwise you will distract the audience.

Use Rule 3 In Organising

Never put too much information on the visual or try and cover too many ideas/concepts on one slide.

Try and limit each slide to one idea and a maximum of three such points. The more you have on a slide, the less impact it will have and the less the audience will remember. Use emphatic and brief T-Shirt slogans or newspaper heading type bullets.

Advance Planning

Identify your main message.
Select the best mode of presentation.
Establish A Timeline

Align the slides to your presentation outline so that they act as memory triggers and become your speaking notes. However, do not use so many visuals that they take the attention away from you.

Reflect your presentation stature (key and sub points) in the headings and sub headings of your slides so that your audience always knows where they are in the structure of your content. The more apparent the structure, the better the attention.

Remember The 3 B's

A visual must be seen by everyone in the audience so the visual must be BIG.

All visual content must be BOLD, meaning that lines must be clear, and not too thin. Clarity is essential so don't use ambiguous shapes or fancy lettering. Avoid using just capital letters in a heading as this is more difficult to read.

Colours must be BRIGHT and contrast well without clashing. Use dark colours on light or clear backgrounds and vice-versa. Use a complimentary colour scheme of not more than 7 colours. 30% of the male population is red/green colour deficient, so be careful not to use these colours together in the same chart or background. Make the "keys" to your graphs large.

Other Tips On Using Visuals

You must lead the visuals, not the other way around. Know the sequence of your slides and their content, so that you can enact a smooth transition from one slide to the next.

Never talk to the visual, always directly face your audience.

If you are going to write or draw anything, make sure that it is neat and clear.

Practice makes perfect! Practice with your visual aid equipment and know exactly how everything works so that you are comfortable and confident in its use.

Remember Murphy's Law and guard against it by being prepared. Have backups and pay attention to detail.

Preparing The Environment

Attend to these physiological factors in order to ensure that the attention of your audience is maintained:

Temperature:

The room should be not too hot or too cold. It is important that you are able to control the temperature of the room you are working in.

Noise:

It is important that the room is noise and disturbance free.

Lighting:

A room that is too light or too dark will have an adverse effect on your presentation.

Ventilation:

It is important that the room is not stuffy or too cold, as this could impact negatively on your presentation.

Comfort Breaks:

Schedule sufficient comfort breaks, and have coffee, tea and water available.

Room Layout:

Arrange the eating so that contact with delegates is maintained and group work and participation is facilitated.

Positioning Of Equipment

It is important that all equipment such as overhead projectors, flipchart stands and videos, are positioned so that all delegates can see them.

In Conclusion

Be Aware Of The Following Pitfalls Of Business Communication:

Too many words
Clichés
Too many big words
Jargon
Vague expressions
Condescending statements
Sexist/racist language

Negative expressions
Inattention to detail
Inattention to the reader
Lack of commitment
Passive construction
Poor grammar
Errors and inaccuracies

www.ingramcontent.com/pod-product-compliance
Lightning Source LLC
Chambersburg PA
CBHW051224170526
45166CB00005B/2037